Smile at the Future

This is an IndieMosh book

brought to you by MoshPit Publishing
an imprint of Mosher's Business Support Pty Ltd

PO Box 4363
Penrith NSW 2750

indiemosh.com.au

Copyright © David Schaeffer 2021

The moral right of the author has been asserted in accordance with the Copyright Amendment (Moral Rights) Act 2000.

All rights reserved. Except as permitted under the Australian Copyright Act 1968 (for example, fair dealing for the purposes of study, research, criticism or review) no part of this publication may be reproduced, stored in a retrieval system, or transmitted in any form or by any means, electronic, mechanical, photocopying, recording or otherwise, without the written permission of the publisher.

 A catalogue record for this work is available from the National Library of Australia

https://www.nla.gov.au/collections

Title:	Smile at the Future
Subtitle:	Finding hope that lasts a lifetime
Author:	Schaeffer, David
ISBNs:	978-1-922542-77-9 (paperback)
	978-1-922542-78-6 (ebook – epub)
	978-1-922542-79-3 (ebook – Kindle)
Subjects:	HISTORY: Modern / General; World;
	SELF HELP: Spiritual; Personal Growth / General.

Cover concept by David Schaeffer and Ariel Tate. Cover design and layout by Ariel Tate. Cover images iStock. Edited by Cathy Geeves, Creative writer/Editor at The Word Haven. Proofread by David Schaeffer, High Endeavours

Smile at the Future

Finding hope
that lasts a lifetime

David Schaeffer

Proverbs 31:25 N.A.S.B
Strength and dignity are her clothing,
and she smiles at the future.

Smile at the Future | v

CONTENTS

INTRODUCTION 1
THE YEAR 2050 3

CREATIVE US 9
    The Technology Revolution 10
    Transportation on Earth 12
    Driverless Vehicles 15
    Transportation In The Air 17
    Transportation In Space 20
    Housing On Earth 24
    Farming And Agriculture 27
    The Changing Workplace 29
    Here Come The Androids 33
    Journalism, Bricklaying And Artificial Intelligence 35

CORRUPT US 37
    Refugees 38
    Human Trafficking 40
    Weaponised Information 43
    Social Media 45
    What's Behind The Screen? 49
    Conspiracy Theories 53
    Some Say Extinction 58
    Prophets Of Secular Society 61
    Will There Be A Church On Future Earth? 62

HOW MUCH TIME DO WE HAVE THIS SIDE OF THE
GRAVE? 67
    Australia's Oldest Person 68

- The Complications Of Ageing 69
- The Increase In Life Expectancy 72
- The World's Blue Zones 74
- Thirsting For The Fountain Of Youth 76

HOW MUCH TIME DO WE HAVE THE OTHER SIDE OF THE GRAVE? 79
- What Most People Believe 80
- The Mystery Of Aging 82
- Hopeful Voices 83
- Serious Research Into The Validity Of Faith-Based Living 85
- Simon Greenleaf - Harvard Law School 86
- Frank Morrison - 'Who Moved The Stone?' 90

SMILING AT THE FUTURE 93
- A Lady Called Wisdom 94
- Meet Prudence 96
- How Did She Become Wise? 99

THE ONLY CONCLUSION THAT MATTERS 103
- Up To You 104

RESOURCES BY DAVID SCHAEFFER 109

DISCLAIMER 111

INTRODUCTION

During the year 2020, a corona virus (specifically known as COVID-19) was sweeping the nations of the earth and transforming the way people live. People began practising 'physical distancing' and a variety of personal hygiene disciplines that only a short time before were considered less necessary. In early February 2021, there were 103,362,039 confirmed cases of COVID-19, including 2,244,713 deaths, reported to World Health Organization. A number of vaccines were developed in record time and the governments of the world were at last able to make significant steps towards bringing this international calamity to heel.

12 months ago, today was the future. Additionally, 12 months ago, no one knew things would turn out as they have. I trust the following thoughts will give you the gift of perspective and that they inspire you to prepare for the future creatively and purposefully.

Apart from alarming calamities like COVID-19, the future could be full of good news. However, a serious flaw in the human race ensures that bad news grabs the majority of local and international news headlines.

The earth has always had its fair share of dreamers. Our history books reveal that over the centuries our smart ideas have taken us to both the heights and depths of achievement. We prove our creativity by building magnificent towers, only to prove how corrupt we are by reducing them to rubble using loaded passenger airliners as agents of destruction. Beautiful marriages and families once dreamed of as 'until death do us part', receive premature death sentences.

In the following pages, we consider what the future will look like and how much of it we have in front of us. We consider both the creativity and the corrupt under belly of the human race. We also take into consideration the prophets of secular society who have no time for God and the prophets of those who do. At the end, we meet a beautiful woman who is smiling at the future; something that many people find hard to do.

My hope for you is that as you enjoy the read, you will ask the right questions, find the right answers and join those of us who are moving confidently into the future.

David Schaeffer

THE YEAR 2050

About 2,500 years ago, a displaced person made the most of his refugee status. He discovered he had an amazing gift that allowed him to see into the future. Cultivating this gift over time, the prophet Daniel saw today's world from afar and prophesied that people would find faster ways to go wherever they were going and they would acquire knowledge at speeds previously unimagined.[1]

Knowing what we do now, let us try and time travel into the future and make some educated guesses about the changes that could occur.

The year is 2050. Global road deaths have been halved to 1640 a day. Driverless vehicles, some electric and others powered by renewable energy sources, now comprise 62% of all privately owned passenger vehicles.

Bill and Melinda Gates' sad predictions that bio-terrorism would be used to wipe out large numbers of the world population, together with their provision of vaccines to prevent infant mortality in third world countries, were two things that contributed to the slowing of world population growth. Third-world families were large because they expected many of their children would die. Gates' intervention lowered both the mortality rate and the numbers of children born to each family. Despite

---
[1] Daniel 12:4

doubling between 1974 and 2018, world population now sits at a manageable 9.8 billion. Predictions that the human race would become extinct and join the list of other species that have, have somewhat subsided.

Olive Trembath, 97, and Hithu Bhatia, her 85-year old neighbour, live in one of Sydney's north-western suburbs. Both have decided to take advantage of the passenger drone supplied by their doctor for their annual flu' shot. They could have driven, but why bother when their age now qualifies them for these benefits? During their short flight, they reminisce about the time when the 'Roads, Maritime and Air Services' was called the 'Roads and Traffic Authority'. They remember with a chuckle how long they would have to queue to obtain a licence renewal. You could spend half your life waiting to be served! Hithu has decided to complete her masters in psychotherapy, considering her life experience and qualifications are suited to this kind of useful occupation. She has become one of the many who have adapted to the 30 or so extra years of life her grandparents did not have. They had a mere life expectancy of '60-something' and would have found '90-something' to be a strange concept.

Sublimely unaware that Uber Air commenced their commercial drone flights in Dallas and Los Angeles in 2023, Olive and Hithu remember back to the 1960s when all of this was the stuff of their eagerly read comic books. As they enjoy their short journey, something similar is happening in Melbourne.

It is Friday afternoon in downtown Melbourne, Australia, where Sarah has agreed to meet Brian on the rooftop of Uber's Skyport. Here they will board their Uber Air passenger drone and fly over Melbourne's rush hour traffic, before landing at Tullamarine Airport for their weekend getaway at Fiji's distinctly slower paced Coral Coast. They are two of 4,000 passengers being ferried at low altitudes across their city every hour. Uber selected the 'beehive' design proposed by Humphreys and Partners back in 2016. Leaving the Skyport, Sarah and Brian's air view of this super structure reminds them of the old pictures their now aged grandparents once showed them from a collection of Star Wars memorabilia.

A continent away and despite their exit from the Royal family, Harry and Meghan (now reinvented as well-known celebrities) have to dash over to London for the day. Harry will attend to some official business and Meghan will wow the crowds at a fashion 'do' that is sponsoring one of their charities. At 4pm, they will meet at the rocket terminal to return home in time for dinner. At almost 12,000kph, their flight from England will take about half an hour.[2] The infamous couple have chosen to fly Virgin Aerospace instead of Musk International as a loyalty to their friend, Richard Branson.

'Spaceclean', a new space junk collection agency, has helped make commercial rocket travel a relatively safe experience for Harry, Meghan and many other excited

---

[2] James Titcombe, The Telegraph, 29 Sept, 2017

travelers. Various recycling centres in America, Russia and China are now re-processing the junk into usable products.

Now in his late 70s, Elon Musk by necessity, has been forced to revise the time frames for some of his mind-boggling projects. He recalls his bold 2017 projection that there could be one million people living on Mars by 2060. Additionally, he remembers that same vision expanding to include humans living on the moon as well as Mars by 2024.[3] Failing to eventuate and despite the disappointment of having to relinquish his personal dream of actually dying on Mars, he draws comfort from the fact that the extensive research and development inspired a race between he and Richard Branson to provide international space travel at commercial rates. On a recent flight, he noticed with sadness that passengers who once used to look out at their beautiful blue planet suspended by invisible forces in a sea of nothing, had already become familiar with space travel and were busily engaging themselves with other things.

Raised and educated in Washington DC, brothers Jacob and Jack Oastler came to New York for work after completing college. Today, they are meeting their friends at New York's Times Square to travel to Washington's FedEx Field, the home ground of their NFL team, the Washington RedWolves. For Jacob and Jack, it has now become a common sight for horizontal doors to suddenly swing downwards and create a neat space where a lift

---

[3] Nadia Drake, National Geographic, Sept 29, 2017

appears with disembarking passengers from one of Musk's Hyperloop stations located 18 metres underground. After entering the lift, they descend and enter a passenger pod. Electromagnetically levitated, the pod hurtles through an intercity tunnel to the sporting venue where they arrive 30 minutes later.

Enough dreaming. Let us return to today.

CREATIVE US

The Technology Revolution

Looking back through recorded history from the year 2020, mankind has experienced a small number of highly visible social revolutions. Until a period of time from approximately 1770 to 1830, the world's societies and economies were largely built on agriculture. In less than a hundred years, life for many was set on a new and revolutionary path as the factories, inventions and machinery of the Industrial Revolution changed the world.

Beginning in the second half of the 1900s, the 'Tech-Rev' with all the trademarks of another genuine worldwide revolution is still sweeping the earth.

Born in Ravensburg, Germany in 1938, Klaus Schwab founded the World Economic Forum, the International Organisation for Public-Private Cooperation, in 1971. At 82 years of age in 2021, he has been at the centre of global affairs for over four decades.

Schwab was convinced that this revolution had the power to fundamentally change the way people lived, worked and related to one another. In his writings, he described ubiquitous, mobile supercomputing, intelligent robots, self-driving cars, neuro-technological brain enhancements and genetic editing. He commented that the evidence of dramatic change was all around and was happening at exponential speed.

His observations concluded that previous social revolutions liberated humankind from animal power, made mass production possible and brought digital capabilities to billions of people. Schwab predicted that this latest Revolution would be characterised by a range of new technologies. These technologies would fuse together the physical, digital and biological worlds impacting all disciplines, economies and industries. Furthermore, they would even challenge the ideas about what it means to be human.

The distinguishing characteristics of the Technology Revolution were, and are, unique.

Previously, there was 'the speed of sound' and 'the speed of light'. The Tech-Rev introduced humanity to 'the speed of now'.[4] Writing in 2015, Klaus Schwab made the following revolutionary statement. "In the new world, it is not the big fish that eats the small fish, it's the fast fish which eats the slow fish.[5]" Speed and reach were arguably the two distinguishing features of this revolution. "And," he continues, "we must learn how to adjust to it or its propensity to increase stress will add to our health problems in unprecedented ways. The resulting shifts and disruptions mean that we live in a time of great promise and great peril.[6]"

---

[4] Dan 12:4

[5] World Economic Forum, 19 Feb, 2015, Klaus Schwab

[6] The Fourth Industrial Revolution, by Klaus Schwab. World Economic Forum

Transportation on Earth

We are actually living through a time in history that will rival the importance of the Industrial Revolution of the late 1700s.

Elon Musk has become one of the world's best known dreamers. Making headlines in 2016 by building his fully electric Tesla Model SP100D production car, it was hailed as the 'quickest production car ever'. In order to make it all possible, electric refuelling stations have started appearing on major road arteries across the world, propelling us forwards with this racy technology. However, it is not thought that every form of transportation will be powered by electricity.

Processed sugar has progressively been labelled an 'official' enemy of the human metabolism. Sugar cane producers in Brazil are aiming at processing sugar for another purpose; the lowest cost carbon fuel in the world to be available in commercial volumes.

The move away from fossil fuels as a primary source of energy saw Royal Dutch Shell and Brazil's Cosan SA Industria e Comercio create a joint venture named 'Raizen'. Raizen is a biofuels company producing almost two billion litres of sugar cane ethanol per year and supplies 5,800 Shell branded service stations in Brazil.[7] Estimates predict that by the year 2050, there will be two

---

[7] Renewablesnow.com, Shell, Cosan make Raizen JV permanent, Nov 24, 2016

billion cars on the planet and fuel consumption will have tripled. Robust discussions between the proponents of fuel powered and electric powered cars continue in their respective boardrooms, and battery recycling is also touted as becoming a major industry by 2025. China and EU carmakers commenced battery recycling in 2020.[8]

In January 2021, Elon Musk's net worth was recorded at $197 billion USD making him the richest man in the world. He continues to push forwards on multiple technology frontiers. 'The Boring Company' was a brainchild of his. Around 2020, he was digging a tunnel under Los Angeles and had received approval to dig under Washington DC. Why? He wanted to build a 150 mph (approximately 240 kph) underground electric vehicle system through tunnels with lifts at each Station. Stations would be no bigger than the lift required to elevate vehicles to ground level before lowering others to commence their journey.[9] For longer distances, there is 'Hyperloop' that aims to allow passengers to travel from London to Edinburgh or Los Angeles to San Francisco in under 30 minutes.

Musk describes Hyperloop as a cross between a Concorde, a railgun and an air hockey table. Based on the very high speed transit (VHST) system proposed in 1972, it combines a magnetically levitating train and a low pressure transit tube. Evolving from some of the original ideas of VHST, it differs in using pods or capsules to move

---

[8] Henry Sanderson, Sept 3, 2017 in The Financial Times Ltd 2018
[9] Jacob Kastrenakes, March 9, 2018, The Verge

from place to place. It was proposed as an alternative to short distance air travel, much faster than existing rail networks and much cleaner than flight. In theory, Hyperloop could go faster, but safety and speed always combine to place limits on high risk projects such as this. In the meantime, there is the advent of the driverless vehicle.

Driverless Vehicles

A driving force behind the push for driverless vehicles is the tragic number of global deaths and injuries. Every year the lives of approximately 1.35 million people are cut short as a result of a road traffic accident. This is an average of 3,700 per day. Sadly, it doesn't stop there. An additional 20 to 50 million are injured or disabled.[10] Ranked as the 9th leading cause of death, this accounted for 2.2% of all deaths globally.

In 2019, the international community was on the verge of seeing the driverless revolution. As this new mode of transport becomes commonplace, some predict that the emotional attachment between owner and vehicle will intensify because of the voice recognition and conversation necessary to set up each trip. Google and Intel have already invested $30 million into the development of driverless vehicles. They purchased the Israeli driverless company, Mobileye, for $15.3 billion[11] and had a sliding scale used for vehicle development. Level 0 referred to a vehicle where the driver had total control. From there, it proceeded through declining amounts of driver control until Level 5 was reached. At Level 5, occupants became purely passengers. Instead of people driving vehicles, the vehicles were now driving them.

---

[10] World Health Organization Feb 7, 2020

[11] Ingrid Lunden, Techcrunch.com, March 13, 2017

The race is becoming more and more competitive between major automotive companies! 2017 saw an enormously important milestone reached, when Waymo began operating self-driving cars on public roads in Phoenix, Arizona.

Audi predicted they would introduce a self-driving car by 2020.[12] U.S software manufacturer, Nu-Tonomy, intended to provide self-driving taxi services in Singapore by 2018 with the plan to expand to 10 cities worldwide by 2020.[13]

Delphi, Mobileye, Ford, Volkswagen, GM, BMW, Toyota, Tesla, Jaguar, Land-Rover and Nissan are all in the race and each predicted their success in quite similar time frames. Expert members of the Institute of Electrical and Electronics Engineers (IEEE) estimated that up to 75% of all vehicles would be driverless by 2040.[14]

---

[12] IEEE Spectrum, 2017-01-0

[13] Yahoo News, 2016-08-29, Digital Trends, 2016-05-24

[14] IEEE, 2012-09-05

Transportation In The Air

On Saturday January 6, 2018, Jennifer Dudley-Nicholson of the Daily Telegraph reported, "Australia has become an international testing ground for commercial drone deliveries. Burritos and medical supplies are expected to descend into backyards this year." By November of the same year, advertisements appeared on Australian television and began the process of gradually 'conditioning' the general public by showing drones dropping bundles of nappies (diapers) into the arms of waiting families. Test Research Company X, previously known as Google X, optimistically predicted that mass deliveries could be five years away. In 2018, the obvious follow on question was, "How long before drones carry people?"

On February 7, 2018, an article in Reuters informed the world that the EHang 184 (an electrically powered human passenger drone) had been tested over 1,000 times in China.[15] It could carry a passenger of less than 100kg and fly at 100kph for 23 minutes at sea level. The city of Dubai announced plans to cooperate with EHang to develop self-flying taxis taking people across the city. The company was eyeing a broader market. Not only able to help people avoid traffic on the ground, their drones could also be used in emergency rescue, the transportation of patients

---

[15] EHang 184, passenger drone makes first public flight in China, Reuters, Updated 7 Feb 2018

to hospital or for use in tourism. EHang co-founder, Derrick Xiong, indicated that the final commercial product could fly into the market possibly within the year.

In January of 2019, a news article appeared stating, "Flying cars are coming sooner than you think."[16]. By the time governments regulate air space for drone deliveries of human or other cargo, the technology will be good to go. This is hailed as a distinct possibility by 2025.

In May 2018, Uber unveiled its new design for an 'electric vertical take-off and landing' vehicle (eVTOL) at the Elevate Summit. The retail giant, Amazon, has already heavily invested in this technology. "We are committed to making our goal of delivering packages by drones in 30 minutes or less a reality," it stated.[17]

Finally, not to be outdone, Toyota's 'SkyDrive' developed and flew their manned SD-03 in August 2020. It is currently the world's smallest electric vertical take off and landing vehicle and takes up the space of two normal sized parked cars.[18]

Finally, there is a possibility that personal flying suits could transport individuals. With no intention of revolutionising human transport, Britain's real life Iron Man, Richard Browning, made headlines in 2018 when he glided down

---

[16] Flying Cars are coming sooner than you think, Adrianna Zappavigna, Jan 1, 2019, News.com.au

[17] Nick Kolakowski, Dec 5, 2018, insights.dice.com

[18] © 2020 Cable News Network, Inc. A WarnerMedia Company. All Rights Reserved. EDT, August 29, 2020

a quiet London street. His original jet suit sold at London's upmarket Selfridges Department Store for $A612,000.00.

Transportation In Space

On December 17, 1903, Orville and Wilbur Wright stood on the threshold of aeronautical innovation when their flying contraption stayed aloft for 59 seconds and covered a distance of 255.6 m (852 ft).

Did Orville turn to Wilbur the night before their maiden voyage and say, "You know, if we survive and get this thing off the ground tomorrow, we could be the reason why flying machines reach the stars in years to come"?

In February 2018, Elon Musk's company Space X launched its reusable 'Falcon Heavy' rocket, a test flight in preparation for commercial travel and colonisation of other moons and planets. Mounted on his rocket, was a Tesla Roadster with a mannequin named 'Starman' sitting behind the wheel. The world watched in amazement as Falcon Heavy soared into space, while two of its three booster rockets separated from the main vehicle and returned to earth. Neatly settling right way up on their landing pads, they were ready for re-use in a never-before-seen manoeuvre. The roadster bearing rocket was to be put on a path around the sun that would slingshot the vehicle out to a distance of Mars' orbit. However, it overshot its trajectory and put Falcon Heavy in an orbit that extended out into the asteroid belt between Mars and Jupiter.

What, by Jupiter, will an unsuspecting alien make of Starman and his rocket-powered roadster when he lands for a pit stop at Falcon Heavy's landing site?

Everyone who pushes a boundary has a motive. The answer to "why did they do it?" can be as simple as, "because we can." Other times it is, "to discover what is out there." Elon Musk appears to have an insatiable appetite for space exploration and human relocation. Why? One reason he provided was that the human race needs saving from itself. His dream to colonise Mars incorporates the idea that when we human beings have finished messing up our life on earth, there would be a remnant left over on the Red planet to carry on. Despite laying claim to a high degree of philanthropic motive to match his gloomy predictions for planet earth and its occupants, there are other probable forces at work driving them forwards. If mankind does not have to evacuate in the predicted time, we would be left with an amazing transportation system benefiting not only the planet, but also that of Musk's insatiable ego and bank account. Probably the biggest reason for 'going at it' is the thrill of doing what no man has done before and an addiction to the wine of thinking without limits.

Musk and the earth's new breed of entrepreneurial space adventurers have spurred NASA on to greater heights. A few hundred years ago, explorers like Christopher Columbus, Vasco da Gama, Ferdinand Magellan and James Cook virtually discovered all there was of Planet Earth. The desire for people to explore the unknown was unstoppable and space exploration has given this urge a new outlet.

Launched on July 30th, 2020, with a hopeful arrival at

the red planet (Mars) in February 2021, the real excitement surrounding NASA's 'Mars2020' mission is that it will carry a drone capable of achieving independent, 'heavier-than-atmosphere' flight. With the wings removed, it is about the size of a softball. Weighing approximately 4 pounds (less than 2 kilos), it is solar-powered and able to fly up to a few hundred metres at a time. The atmosphere on Mars is less than 1 per cent as dense as the Earth's and flying on the surface of Mars is equivalent to flying 100,000 feet above sea level on earth. To compensate for the thin air, the drone's wings are engineered to spin at 10 times the normal rate to achieve lift.[19]

Of course, getting there is always a problem that begins just beyond the earth's atmosphere. In the 1950s, Russia and America began sending rockets into space. Since then, we have left a trail of trash behind us. A vast amount of 'space junk' is orbiting the Earth, traveling at speeds up to 17,500 mph (28,163 kph). The burned out and split off 'thingamejiggers' actually move fast enough to cause serious damage to any slightly off course satellite or spacecraft.[20] In January 2017, the European Space Agency's Space Debris Office located in Darmstadt, Germany was tracking, correlating and cataloguing 29,000 objects larger than 10 cm, 750,000 from 1 to 10 cm, and more than 166 million from 1 mm to 1 cm.

---

[19] Brian Resnick, Vox.com, May 14, 2018

[20] National Aeronautics and Space Administration. Page Last updated Aug 7, 2017. Official: Brian Dunbar

Every day a tonne or two of defunct satellites, rocket parts and other man-made orbiting junk hurtles into earths atmosphere. Four-fifths of it burns up to become harmless dust.

Housing On Earth

Back on earth, those two billion cars in use by 2050 represent a significant rise in world population. What kind of dwellings and communities will be available for these people to live in? Creative minds are grappling with the challenges to design cities and population centres that reflect future needs.

Abu Dhabi, located in the United Arab Emirates, was built during the 1900s in a western way. It is today powered by what was previously considered to be unlimited oil reserves. Air conditioners, bitumen roads and fuel-guzzling vehicles all contribute to massive energy bills. On any 39C degree day, the heat coming from the asphalt there is 57 degrees Celsius.

On the outskirts of Abu Dhabi city, construction began in 2008 on a revolutionary project. Situated right next to the International Airport, the 1,483-acre Masdar City was hailed as a (not quite) Utopian City rising out of the desert.

Carbon neutral, pedestrian friendly and mostly powered by renewable energy sources, it was a statement for the future. A most amazing feature of this city is that its entire transportation system is electric and underground. This allows buildings to be built closer to each other providing more shade for pedestrians. In addition, solar panels atop buildings cast more shadows to assist in reducing the daytime temperatures. With the city built around pedestrians rather than a transport system, ground temperatures are normally 33 degrees Celsius compared with Abu Dhabi's 57 degrees. Air conditioning needs have been reduced by 60% thanks (in part) to a law preventing glass windows receiving direct sunlight.[21]

Some principles from a city like this in desert temperatures, can be modified for many other climates. Not to be outdone, Saudi Arabia has plans too.

[22]Four months after becoming the Crown Prince of Saudi Arabia, Mohammed bin Salman announced his intention to build a $US500 billion futuristic megacity. Located near the northern region of the Red Sea, it will be 33 times the size of New York City.

Named Neom, the city is intended to be carbon neutral and have artificial rain. Early blueprints drawn up by consultants also state that Neom would have a fake moon, flying taxis, robotic maids and holographic teachers. It has been since branded as a future hub for pioneering clean energy development. A key part of 'Vision 2030,' the project is the Prince's plan to modernise the kingdom and shed its reliance on petrodollars amid fluctuating oil prices. Despite Covid19 slowing their progress, Vision 2030 is pushing towards its original deadline.

In an alternate conceptualisation, the world in 2018 boasted its own approved 'Earthship Academy' where

---

[21]BBC Documentary "The World in 2050 (The Real Future of Earth), 2018

[22]Business Insider Australia, Bill Bostock, 24 September 2020

growing numbers of environmentally concerned earthlings have inspired changed building codes. Tyres, bottles and a host of throw away items[23] have now been approved as construction materials for (mostly) self-sustaining dwellings.

Michael Reynolds and a staff of top Earthship builders, electricians, plumbers and plant specialists have now trained over 1,400 students from around the world at their Biotecture Academy. Dividing the classes into smaller groups, the instructors work on a variety of aspects such as pounding earth into tyres, can and bottle wall construction, adobe mud pack out and plaster, carpentry, roofing, glazing and independent power and water systems. On becoming accredited, they commenced an official partnership with the University of Western Colorado.

---

[23] https://www.earthshipglobal.com/

Farming And Agriculture

Brilliant minds are finding ways to adapt and prepare for the needs of the future. The human race needs to eat, and agriculture is the earth's most necessary and oldest practice. Rod Kater's old beef property is known as 'Bonnington'. Situated at Allynbrook beneath the long shadow of the Barrington Tops and located north west of Newcastle in New South Wales, Bonnington has been the site of some interesting experiments.[24] In the Twenty-teens, Dr. Rod and his wife Penny were involved in some very interesting research that played a part in changing the nature of agriculture. Rather than employing more humans to do the heavy lifting, they collaborated with Professor Salah Sukkarieh at the Australian Centre for Field Robotics, Sydney University. Rod was considering robots as his new farmhands.

An early prototype, 'Swagbot' is an ungainly four-wheeled robot capable of moving quietly through a herd calling out "car-morn ... car-morn" (come on) and providing feed for hungry Aberdeen Angus cattle. The ungainly vehicle resembled what one might imagine a crater skirting lunar vehicle to be.

There is also good news for market gardeners. Professor Sukkarieh's workshop in Sydney is also in the process of inventing machines like 'Digital Farmhand' and 'Ripper'.

---

[24] ABC program Catalyst, Series 18, Farmer Needs a Robot

These two robots are being designed to have numerous implements attached to them and they promise vegetable growers relief from hours of backbreaking work. These forward thinking strategists are preparing to meet the worldwide need for 'more food grown smarter'.

The Changing Workplace

In 2018, The World Economic Forum compiled a report by surveying 313 business executives, who together represented 15 million employees around the world. It stated, "By 2022, 42% of task hours will be performed by machines and 58% by people."[25]

Written in 2017, 'Future Brain' by Dr. Jenny Brockis compared a standard working week to an extinct dinosaur. The technology revolution, the information age, increasing globalisation and constant interaction with overseas marketplaces have become shaping tools for the new workplace.

The development of the virtual workplace has seen a definite swing away from office locations and traditional working hours. And with this comes certain advantages. For example, professionally qualified mums-at-home can be brought back to the workforce, receiving not only the benefit of a job, but still having a life as well.

Consider this real life scenario from 2020. Hugh, an Australian, lives in Finland and works from home. He is employed by a Company based in the United Kingdom and analyses international sporting fixtures across different time zones.

In the 2020s, the world is not waiting for a new age to

---

[25] Hamza Shaban, Sept 19, 2018, Washington Post

dawn. We are either keeping up or slipping behind and the new workplace is characterised by new dynamics.

Presenteeism, a current problem in the old workplace could be seriously reduced. Presenteeism refers to the productivity lost when an employee turns up for work, but works at a lower capacity due to illness, or some form of depression. As a reflection of what the human race has been doing to itself, depression has become one of the leading causes of workplace disability.

In 2016, Pathology Awareness Australia commissioned a report from the Centre for International Economics. The report estimated that sick workers dragging themselves into the office are costing the Australian economy more than $34 billion a year.[26] Compared to this, absenteeism was costing the economy less at $24 billion.[27]

Working from home with greater flexibility could go some of the way to alleviating this problem.

Some have likened the current trends in the workplace to how people lived before the Industrial Revolution began in the 1700s. Before large factories were built, people were creating their own working environments.

'Say goodbye to long commutes, office politics and the nine-to-five grind—if you haven't already. According to The Freelancer's Union, one in three Americans (roughly

---

[26] Lucy Carter, for ABC News and HRM, 12th April, 2016

[27] Introduction, The Future Brain, Dr. Jenny Brockis. First published by John Wiley and Sons Australia Ltd

42 million) is an independent worker. And, by 2020, many predict that freelancers will make up 50% of the labour force'.[28]

This trend is extending across many nations. Technology, the Internet and a desire for a better lifestyle is contributing to this major shift in workplace dynamics.

According to research conducted by Forbes, jobs with the brightest futures include healthcare, retail sales, food preparation and customer service. These are occupations where actual people are unlikely to be replaced by machines. And why? Because humans will always need to care for others and will always want others to care about them. Robots will never replace the need humans have for warm, thoughtful and enriching relationships, both personal and professional.

In 2020, we were given a glimpse of the changing workplace when the virus COVID-19 took hold of the world by its jugular vein. The rate of anticipated change received a shot of adrenalin. [29]In a matter of weeks, vibrant cities were turned into virtual ghost towns. Office blocks were vacated, public transport dwindled, and employees were sent home with laptops and other communication devices. An almost immediate cultural change was forced onto the workplace as home became the new office for tens of thousands. In Australia, 24.6 million people were told to stay at home unless they

---

[28] Micha Kaufman, Forbes, Feb 28, 2014

[29] Gian De Poloni, ABC News, 11 April 2020

absolutely had to go outside. This was almost the entire Australian population.

Julian Bolleter, Co-Director of the Australian Urban Design Research Centre, said he expected a sustained cultural shift towards working from home even after the pandemic had passed.

"I think it has forced a lot of organisations to work online, even though the technology has been around for some time," he said. "We won't be the same again and people will adapt to this new way of working."

"A final word," he said. "Take a deep breath and get ready for the 2020s being the era of massive change. 2020 has started with a bang as far as COVID-19 is concerned and it's going to be an era of significant change.

It has killed off the old economy. Let's start again. Let's do it better."[30]

---

[30] Peter Newman, Professor of Sustainability, Curtin University

Here Come The Androids

During the Twenty-teens, Japanese 'bad boy' inventor Hiroshi Ishiguro described himself as the 'father' (not inventor) of his advanced android, Erica. He described her as the 'most beautiful, human-like and autonomous android in this world'. Clearly, he became emotionally over invested despite her being a machine he had personally invented. He designed her to technically evolve in a way that made her appear to crave human interaction. She could tell jokes and have aspirations. The silicone-skinned robot could not move her arms, but she could localise where sound was coming from and unnervingly identify who she was talking to.[31] Despite claims that Erica had a soul, future owners would undoubtedly twig to that fallacy each time they reached for the switch that turned her off and on.

In 2016, 'Sophia' was created by David Hanson, a Disney imagineer. Created in part after Audrey Hepburn and Hanson's wife, Sophia rocketed to stardom. She sat for TV interviews, appeared on the cover of Elle magazine and was appointed the UN's first non-human innovation champion.

But, stop the clock! (if possible). Sophia and Erica's technology were quickly superseded. Humanoid robots began being categorised as 'traditional' and 'modern'. In 2018, NASA put out a call for innovators to develop soft

---

[31] Ben Graham, news.com.au, Dec 4th 2017

robotic technologies. Rebecca Kramer-Bottiglio and her team at Yale University responded by developing robotic skins made of pliable elastic sheets. Kramer-Bottiglio and her team wrapped this intelligent skin around the legs of a soft toy horse and it lurched forwards in an awkward gallop. A foam tube wrapped with a robotic skin was able to inch forward like a worm. A piece of 'skilicone' connecting two pieces of cardboard could contract, turning the object into a rudimentary gripper.[32]

By late 2018, China had become the world leader in robotic research and development. One creation appeared on television as a humanoid Chinese newsreader with a slightly robotic voice. Developed by State News Agency, Xinhua, and tech firm, Sogou Inc., the artificially intelligent robot anchorman almost perfectly mimicked human facial expressions and mannerisms.

Of course, this is old technology according to Elon Musk, who in 2020 was promising to develop Neuralink[33] brain implants. This proposed technology sows a computer chip into the brain on a network of superfine electrode-studded wires. In his mind, this project is meant to achieve symbiosis and 'juice-up' mankind's brain power. If all goes well, he could help medical science make advances with the use of prosthetic limbs. As improbable as it seems, we applaud his never ending capacity to dream.

---

[32] Nick Lunn, Science Robotics, September 19, 2018

[33] Wired, Head Start, August 28, 2020

Journalism, Bricklaying And Artificial Intelligence

In 2019, a news reader asked,[34] "Can robots write news? It turns out they already are. In the Wired article 'What News-Writing Bots Mean for the Future of Journalism,' Joe Keohane explained how Heliograph and other artificial intelligence were writing data-heavy stories about sports and election results."

Heliograph was owned by the Washington Post, which in turn was purchased by the CEO of Amazon, Jeff Bezos. Bezos bought the Post in 2013 when artificially intelligent news writing was in its infancy. Heliograph got its start auto-publishing articles during the Rio 2016 Olympics.

In another field of robotic development, Hadrian X would never win a beauty contest. Who would have guessed that human bricklayers would be replaced? In 2020, resembling a one-armed Tyrannosaurus Rex, this wheezing hydraulic beast and its improved versions are threatening to transform this age-old occupation. Perth based Fastbrick Robotics were getting almost too many enquiries about its new house-building machine. The machine required minimal human interaction and worked day and night, laying up to 1,000 bricks an hour—about the output of two human bricklayers for a day.[35]

Our collective creativity is a sight to behold and makes

---

[34] Heidi Larson, Columnist, BG Falcon Media, Apr 9, 2018

[35] Chris Pash, Financial Review, Oct 2 2017

one wonder what other amazing achievements human beings are capable of. Whilst there seems to be no end to this river of brilliance, we have a frustrating downside to this glorious attribute. This downside erodes our worth as surely as a windstorm strips away topsoil from prime farming land. As creative as humanity is, we have an undeniably corrupt side that blights and erodes; that turns celebration to dismay and causes us to wonder how these two opposites come to dwell in the same space. And so, we must address the flip side of our creativity.

CORRUPT US

Refugees

We have all seen images where streams of people are fleeing their famine or war-torn countries, parking at armed borders of neighbouring countries seeking refuge. Some with all their earthly possessions in a wheelbarrow. Crowds can be seen fighting to receive supplies from United Nations relief vehicles. Médecins Sans Frontières are in their midst with their makeshift aid centres. Everywhere, people are seen drinking from whatever water supply they can find.

One in every 113 people on the planet was a refugee as at June 2017. Around the world, someone was displaced every three seconds, forced from their homes by violence, war, natural disasters or persecution.[36] Midway through 2017, the number of displaced people in the world had risen to 65.6 million. That is more than the population of the United Kingdom. Of the nearly 22.5 million refugees among them, over half were under the age of 18.

The number had increased by 300,000 from the year before. It was the largest number ever recorded according to the UN Refugee Agency, UNHCR. By June 2018, the number of refugees hit a 'five year worldwide high'[37] with more than 68 million people having fled their homes.

Most displaced persons are as damaged as the country or

---

[36] unhcr.org, 19 June 2017

[37] Lauren Said–Moorhouse, CNN, Updated 1:01 AM EDT June 19, 2018

situation he or she was torn from. Finding them a new home is far more than a logistical relocation exercise when their emotional trauma is factored in. Although some governments and world leaders were truly concerned, the size of the challenge is proving to be way beyond the understanding and ability of humankind. This could be one humanitarian problem the human race will never have enough human resources to fix.

Human Trafficking

In the late 1700s and early 1800s, England's William Wilberforce and many others who were appalled at slavery, awakened the consciousness of Great Britain and America by asking the question, "Should one human being have the right to own another human being?" Though they fought and won an exhaustingly long battle, slavery has reared its ugly head again and again. In the late twenty-teens, the United Nations Office on Drugs and Crime (UNODC), collected data from 155 countries and compiled its Global Report on Trafficking in Persons.[38]

According to the report, the most common form of human trafficking then (79%) was sexual exploitation. The victims of sexual exploitation were (and still are) predominantly women and girls. Surprisingly, in 30% of the countries that provide information on gender, women made up the largest proportion of traffickers. In some parts of the world, women trafficking women was the norm. Worldwide, almost 20% of all trafficking victims were children. Men, women and children were trafficked for a wide range of exploitive purposes, such as servitude, slavery, forced labour, debt bondage, forced marriage or organ harvesting. World Vision estimates that nearly 21 million people are being trafficked for profit each year.

---

[38] https://www.unodc.org/unodc/en/human-trafficking/global-report-on-trafficking-in-persons.html

How Young are the Victims of Human Trafficking?

[39]In the summer of 2015, the Centre for Medical Progress in America released videos exposing the sale of baby body parts. These undercover videos showed Planned Parenthood staff discussing abortion procedures with individuals they believed to be interested in buying baby body parts for research. These videos kicked off a national awareness of the gruesome process of trading in baby body parts and even the potential for babies to be born alive and harvested for research. This awakening led to the birth of the Born Alive Abortion Survivors Protection Act.

The undercover work of the Centre for Medical Progress reveals a cynical culture of disregard for human foetuses by high-level executives and senior abortion performers in Planned Parenthood (PP). In fact, some Planned Parenthood sites were revealed to be knowingly conducting illegal trade in human foetal tissue with commercial buyers. However, what is most troubling about the revelation of the CMP tapes is the recorded abortion providers' bland attitudes towards aborted foetuses as faceless commodities for sale. In some cases, for personal benefit, the trade takes place without any expressed sense of compassion or concern for either the aborted infants or their mothers.

In 2017, the LA Times reported that two related

---

[39] Charlotte Lozier Institute, Use of Aborted Fetal Tissue: Questions and Answers, June 5, 2019

companies in California, DaVinci Biosciences and DV Biologics "reached a $7.785-million settlement with the Orange County district attorney's office over allegations that they illegally sold foetal tissue to companies around the world." The same companies were featured in the CMP tapes for sourcing foetal tissue from Planned Parenthood. "The agreement also required the companies to admit liability for violations of state and federal laws prohibiting the sale or purchase of foetal tissue for research purposes."

In 2018, the leading cause of death worldwide was abortion. According to the World Health Organisation, an astonishing 40 to 50 million children are killed before birth.[40] This corresponds to approximately 125,000 each day. By contrast, 8.2 million people died from cancer, 5 million from smoking and 1.7 million from HIV/AIDS.

---

[40] Worldometers

Weaponised Information

We all know that while the Internet can be used for good and gain, it can also be used for harm. 'Weaponised information' is a relatively new term for a very ancient practice. The term was invented to reflect one of the most dangerous elements of our corrupt nature. Examples of it like 'Cambridge Analytica' were not hard to find.

In 2018, Mark Zuckerberg, CEO of Facebook, was accused of failing to protect Facebook users' data. It emerged that 50 million user records had been improperly siphoned off to the political consultancy firm Cambridge Analytica. And why? There were people and organisations in the world who wanted to influence and manipulate the way the masses thought, felt and chose.

And what a grasp Ivy Wigmore has on Weaponised Information![41] The consulting and Content Editor with Tech-Target, she lived on beautiful Prince Edward Island. A maritime province of Eastern Canada, the island was made most famous to the wider world by Anne of Green Gables. She wrote,

"Weaponised information is a message or content piece that is designed to affect the recipient's perception about something or someone in a way that is not warranted. The term implies a target and the intention to cause harm.

---

[41] "weaponized information," posted by Margaret Rouse, Contributor: Ivy Wigmore, WhatIs.com, updated August 2017

The goal of Weaponised Information is (to bring) about a change in beliefs and attitudes and, as a result, promote behaviour that serves the attacker's purpose. Attacks involving Weaponised Information are sometimes referred to as cognitive hacking.

Weaponised Information often consists of intentional falsehoods, known as disinformation. It can also be true but taken out of context, like a comment carefully selected from a longer statement so that it does not reflect what the speaker said. It may be a mixture of truth and lies, so that the known facts lend credence to the untruths. In other cases, the information may be true but its significance overblown or the timing of release calculated to cause the most harm possible.

Propaganda is an example of Weaponised Information: misleading or biased information of a political nature that is usually spread by governments. In contrast, Weaponised Information is also used in the marketplace to gain a competitive advantage. It might be used to tarnish a competitor's reputation, for example, or spread fear, uncertainty and doubt (FUD) about a product or technology. Weaponised Information is one form of social engineering. The presentation of the information may be skillfully crafted to exploit common cognitive biases and errors. People can protect themselves from being affected by Weaponised Information by strengthening their capacity for critical thinking."

Of course, mankind's brilliance can be applied to corrupt or creative thinking. Social media is a classic example.

Social Media

The information age and social networking has changed forever the way human beings communicate with each other. Physical research used to be carried out in libraries, but libraries are now online and the distributed intelligence from the internet is referred to as the 'Global Brain.'[42] This Global Brain plays the role of a nervous system for the social super organism.

With the immense volume of information at our fingertips and the speed at which we can send and receive any number of communications, there still remains a downside to the creative genius of the technology revolution.

Marilyn Price-Mitchell, PhD writes:

[43]"In the past several years, more studies have linked social media to poor mental health. According to a recent Forbes article, several studies have not only shown a correlation, but also a causation. Findings suggest that people who limit social media to 30 minutes daily feel significantly better than those who use social media for longer periods of time. By reducing time spent, people were able to reduce depression, anxiety, and loneliness."

---

[42] Francis Heylighen, Marta Lenartowicz, Technological Forecasting and Social Change, Jan 2017, pp1-6

[43] Marilyn Price-Mitchell, PhD, Disadvantages of Social Networking: Surprising Insights from Teens, Roots of Action, Sept 6th, 2019

She lists ten disadvantages of social networking after beginning her article with the following quote. At first glance, you may think it could come from a parent or grandparent lamenting the harm social networking is perpetrating on their children and grandchildren.

"Honestly, I sometimes truly wish that 'tools' such as the iPhone (or any smartphone), laptops, iPads, tablets, etc. hadn't been invented. Sure, they're great, incredibly useful, and fun time-killers. But the way teenagers abuse them and turn them into mini social control rooms is frankly awful."

However, the author of the quote was a Seattle-area tenth grader, writing an assignment to answer the question, "How has online social networking influenced your relationships with friends and family?"

This student goes on to write, "The teenage way of life has completely changed from what it was only 20 years ago. Now, there is a dramatic decrease in face-to-face communication, which reduces our generation's ability to interact with others on a speaking level."

Amongst the disadvantages she lists are "Gives people a license to be hurtful, creates a skewed self-image and reduces family closeness."

No parent wants their teenage children manipulated, but after a few decades of technological development, online manipulation is now occurring within the four walls of our homes. In 2006–2008, experiments began with a view to creating social mobile networks. These became widely adopted in 2008–2009. Smart phones appeared and suddenly our devices were capable of so much more than telephone calls.

Now, an adolescent is able to take a 'selfie' and be deluged with comments about their self-image. It matters what others think of us, but are we meant to know what *hundreds* of others think of us? Are we meant to receive a constant stream of social approval or criticism?

Adolescents are particularly vulnerable. It is easy for them to interpret others' perceptions of them as truth.

Until 2010/2011 in North America, the number of teenage girls being admitted to hospital for self-harm was stable. Afterwards it escalated dramatically. Self-harm in older teen girls (15-19) rose by 62%. Self-harm in girls between the ages of 10 and 14 rose by 189%. Suicide in older teen girls rose by 70%, and in 10 to14-year-olds, it rose by 151%.[44]

What people do on their screens, (particularly adolescents), is messing with their hormones. Particularly dopamine. Dopamine is referred to as the 'motivation molecule' and is a hormone released in the brain when we expect a reward. Here is a typical scenario.

- An alert sounds on our device indicating information has arrived.

---

[44] Jonathan Haidt, PhD, NYU Stern School of Business, Social Psychologist, Author, The Righteous Mind: Why Good people Are Divided by Politics and religion. Contributor to The Social Dilemma, Argent Pictures

- We experience a release of dopamine, motivating us to pull away from what we were doing and receive the reward of discovering what just arrived.
- Over time, it becomes an automatic response to instantly put life on hold and respond to the alert that sounds on our device.
- With constant stimulation, our dopamine supply runs low. Over time, many people develop *Dopamine Deficiency Syndrome*.
- In our jaded condition we send a note to our friends informing them that we are taking a break from social media.
- A short time later, an emotional attraction compels us to return to the same vicious cycle.

Has humanity, unable to resist the temptation, been conditioned to use their devices as pacifiers? Is this healthy?

What's Behind The Screen?

Imagine a one-way mirror in an interview room at a police station. Behind the mirror, looking in at the person being interviewed is a team of highly qualified people. They are listening to every word, observing every detail of body language and formulating their next most effective approach to the person of interest.

Now, in your imagination, replace the one-way mirror with a screen so small it can fit on your wrist or in your pocket, or so large it can fit into a monitor as large as a TV screen.

Behind those screens are teams of highly qualified social engineers and highly sophisticated super computers. They are busy gathering and recording every interaction you have on your devices. Using binary logarithms, these computer systems calculate every time we 'click' or 'like' or 'send' etc, and they also record how long we spend looking at whatever it is that interests us.

Over time, behind our screens, a model of us is being systematically compiled containing our likes, interests, preferences and personality. Each time we use any of our social media platforms like Facebook, Google and Twitter, another piece of our picture is added. Why is this happening?

Because large Internet Companies are competing with each other for our time and attention. And the better they are at getting our attention, the more other Companies choose to advertise with them. And today, Internet Companies are the richest Companies in the history of the world.

From the 1960's to 2020, computer processing power has increased about a trillion times. What a remarkable achievement in this field of endeavour! Other fields of development such as transport, education, medicine etc. are progressing at a snail's pace in comparison.[45] Should we be applauding? Or should we be worried? Both, but there are sinister forces at play.

Nowhere, other than what is happening behind the screens of our communication and entertainment devices, has the human race demonstrated its ability to simultaneously create and corrupt. But some are beginning to object to the downside of internet communications, and their objections are coming from the very heart of the technology revolution.

A growing army of ethicists, computer scientists, former Google, Twitter, YouTube and Facebook executives, university PhD's and social engineers are now sounding an alarm. Many of these people were enthusiastic proponents of social engineering but have now switched sides.[46] Here are some of their findings.

---

[45] Randima (Randy) Fernando. NVIDIA Former Product Manager, Mindful Schools Former Executive Director, Center for Humane Technology Co-Founder

[46] Contributors on the Documentary 'The Social Dilemma,' Argent Pictures, An Exposure Labs Production

- Social engineers and super-computers are constantly working to make what appears on our screens, more and more addictive. They are constantly working to produce gradual, slight, imperceptible changes in us by what we view on our screens. – *Jaron Linier, Founding father of Virtual Reality, Computer Scientist*
- Social engineers work for those who want to advertise. Advertising has evolved from presenting products to us in their best light in the *hope* that we will make a purchase, to modifying our attitudes and ideas so that we will *want* to make a purchase. – *Justin Rosenstein, Facebook Former Engineer, Google Former Engineer, Asana Co-Founder*
- Computer models of us are being built to predict our actions. Whoever has the best model, attracts the best advertisers and wins. – *Aza Raskin, Firefox and Mobile Labs, Center for Humane Technology Co-Founder, Inventor Infinite Scroll*
- We (social engineers) have created an entire global generation who have and are being manipulated to think and communicate about things that are generated by processes behind the screen. Deceit and sneakiness is at the centre of everything we do. – *Jaron Linier, Founding father of Virtual Reality, Computer Scientist.*
- There are teams of engineers whose job it is to hack people's psychology. The aim was and is to

make computer engineers into behaviour change geniuses. – *Tristan Harris: Google Former Design Ethicist, Center For Humane Society Co-Founder.*
- Constant research and testing helped companies like Facebook and Google to get users to do what they want them to do. *It is manipulation. – Sandy Parakilas. Facebook Former Operations Manager, Uber Former Product Manager*
- These companies discovered they could affect real world behaviour and emotions without ever triggering the user's awareness. They (the users) are completely clueless. – *Shoshana Zuboff, PhD. Harvard Business School, Professor Emeritus, Author: The Age of Surveillance Capitalism.*
- 'There are only 2 industries that call their customers users: Illegal drugs and software.' – *Edward Tufte.*
- It is normally concluded that adults are self-determining individuals. Is this still the case? – *Author.*
- The common question regarding artificial intelligence is "when will machines become smarter than people?" The bigger and more important question is, "when did artificial intelligence successfully begin exploiting human weakness?"

Conspiracy Theories

A conspiracy theory is a theory that explains an event or set of circumstances as the result of a secret plot, usually by powerful conspirators.[47]

It is commonly accepted that these theories thrive in an atmosphere of uncertainty, fear and anxiety, however the Information Age provides another reason. Conspiracy theories can also flourish by virtue of the deluge of material that arrives uninvited on our communication devices courtesy of massive super computers behind our screens. And it appears to most of us that there are more in existence than ever before. But this is not the case.

Historical data[48]

'There are no major comprehensive, longitudinal studies on attitudes toward conspiracy theories, mostly because it was not rigorously measured until about 10 to 20 years ago.

However, researchers have done a considerable amount of work in recent years in an attempt to understand this apparent phenomenon.

Political scientists Joseph E. Uscinski and Joseph M. Parent reviewed over 120 years of letters to the editor, from 1890 to 2010, for both The New York Times and the Chicago Tribune.

---

[47] Merriam-Webster Dictionary

[48] Live Science. 'Are Conspiracy Beliefs on the Rise?' by Liberty Vittert – Washington University of St Louis, September 20, 2019

In over 100,000 letters, this review showed absolutely no change in the amount of conspiracy theory belief over time. In fact, the percent of letters about conspiracy theories actually declined from the late 1800s to the 1960s and has remained steady since then.

While these researchers looked at data only up until 2010, current polling has not shown any increase in conspiracy theory belief since then.'

'In 1964, the New York Times said conspiracy theories had grown weed-like in this country.

In 1994, the Washington Post declared it to be the dawn of a new age of conspiracy theory.

In 2004, the Boston Globe stated that we are in the golden age of conspiracy theory.'

Then in 2008 and 2009, social mobile networking flooded our smart phones, and whilst the number of conspiracy theories did not noticeably increase, the readership of those being broadcast did. The consequence was an increased number of 'believers.'

Nine percent of the North American population believed in 'Pizzagate,' the theory that Washington elite engaged in child sex trafficking at the basement of a D.C. pizzeria.

Nineteen percent of North Americans believe that the government is using chemicals to control the population.

Some quite educated people subscribe enthusiastically to the notion, popular in the dark ages, that planet earth is flat, not round.

There is another theory that says the earth is hollow and that there might even be a whole other civilization of advanced beings living in it.

One conspiracy theory claimed 5G's millimetre wave technology was secretly developed by governments as a weapon to threaten and control people.

Another conspiracy linked 5G to the emergence of COVID-19, claiming coronavirus was deliberately released so 5G could be rolled out without opposition while communities were in lockdown.

Conspiracy theories have people discussing them like never before. Could it be that once, when we casually or even accidentally clicked on a certain topic on the internet, algorithmically-minded super computers went to work, generating bundles of information and disinformation about that topic to our screens? Have our minds been manipulated? Could it be that computer technology and social engineering rather than the conspiracy theories themselves should be our primary source of concern?

Two conclusions in the face of this information are:

- Parents must firstly educate themselves regarding these matters. They should set values in the home that will positively impact their children's journey to adulthood. Perhaps the best parents will introduce their children to sport and the great outdoors, protecting them from the addictive forces at play through their screens.

- Parents should educate their children. One definition of the word discernment' is 'telling the difference.' Teenagers must understand what is going on behind their screens, and they should be encouraged to develop a healthy capacity for discernment. Parents should turn all outside communication off during meal times and lead their children in conversations that role-model critical thinking.

A final word. During the 20th Century, two famous books were written in an attempt to predict the future. They were written as novels and both were dystopian. That is, they described an imaginary place or condition that is as bad as possible. The first was written in 1931 by Aldous Huxley and was called *Brave New World.* The second was written in 1949 by George Orwell and bore the title, *1984.*

Neil Postman, in his highly regarded work *Amusing Ourselves to Death,* compares the large differences proposed by each author.

- Orwell warns that we will be overcome by an externally opposed oppression.
- Huxley's vision requires no Big Brother. As he saw it, people would come to love their oppression, to adore the technologies that would undo their capacities to think.
- Orwell feared that the truth would be concealed from us and that we would become a captive culture.
- Huxley feared that we would be drowned in a sea of information and become a trivial culture.

- In short, Orwell feared that what we hated would ruin us.
- Huxley feared that what we loved would ruin us.[49]

Both were right to a significant degree. Orwell painted a clear picture of peoples' lives under totalitarian regimes. Huxley painted a picture that clearly resembles the larger part of the world in the 21st Century.

Once again, the human race demonstrates its ability to simultaneously create and corrupt. Some think we are so corrupt that we are on a collision course with extinction.

---

[49] pp11-12, '2084– Artificial Intelligence and the Future of Humanity' by John C Lennox, Zondervan Publishers.

Some Say Extinction

On March 14, 2018, Stephen Hawking's mortal life came to an end. His poor body succumbed to the ravages of neuromuscular wasting, a condition known as Lou Gehrig's disease. Sadly, he had spent over 40 years in a wheelchair. In 2016, he predicted humanity would become extinct in 1,000 years; i.e. by the year 3016. A year later, he made a much more alarming prediction. The cosmologist, physicist and atheist predicted that the human species would have to populate a new planet within 100 years, i.e. by the year 2116, to ensure its survival.[50]

Needless to say, not everyone thought like Hawking.

Michael Guillen Ph. D, first met Stephen Hawking at Harvard around 1987. The following year, shortly after the publication of Hawking's first book 'A Brief History of Time', he allowed Guillen to interview him for ABC News.

In his opinion, this new prediction of 100 years indicated a serious flaw in Hawking's thinking. He did not consider that Hawking's marbles had been rearranged, however he did suspect he had 'become the Donald Trump of science, given to saying outrageous things for the fun of it and to attract attention'. Guillen stated that Hawking's predictions were spectacularly unscientific and that his prophecy was also wrongheaded. "Let's see if I have this

---

[50] Kate O'Malley, May 8, 2017, Elle

right: we have trashed the earth – with the help of science, I might add, given that he asserts technology-gone-wrong is part of our current mess – so now what? Earth be damned, we must save our own hides, and quickly?"[51]

At 80 years of age, Sir David Attenborough was on the same page as Hawking. With a hint of exasperation, he stated that the human race had become "a plague on the Earth. It is coming home to roost over the next 50 years or so. It's not just climate change; it is sheer space and places to grow food for this enormous horde. Either we limit our population growth or the natural world will do it for us."[52]

Eminent Australian scientist Professor Frank Fenner, who helped wipe out smallpox, also agreed with Hawking and predicted humans would probably be extinct within 100 years. This belief was based on the effects of overpopulation, environmental destruction and climate change.[53]

Writing for Live Science in 2010, Wynne Parry had a vastly different take on the future. He predicted the earth could continue to host life for another 1.75 to 3.25 billion years, as long as nuclear holocaust, an errant asteroid or some other disaster didn't intervene.[54]

---

[51] Opinion, Michael Guillen, Fox News May 8,2017 PhD

[52] Louise Gray, Environment Correspondent, 22 Jan 2013, The Telegraph

[53] June 23, 2010 by Lin Edwards, Phys.org report (The Australian)

[54] Wynne Parry | September 18, 2013, Live Science, "How Much Longer Can Earth Support Life?"

The ongoing extinction of species on earth is a well-documented process. Those that believe the human race is drawing closer to its own extinction propose gargantuan guess-like statistics such as 'more than 90 per cent of all species that arose since life began on Earth 3.8 billion years ago are extinct'.[55] If people are not careful, they will swallow these scientific-sounding statements as facts without asking if they are legitimate science.

The commonly held definition of science is:

'The systematic study of the nature and behaviour of the material and physical universe based on observation, experiment, and measurement, and the formulation of laws to describe these facts in general terms'.

Systematic study? Observation? Experiment and measurement? 3.8 billion years ago? Hmmm. It should be pointed out that what has been served up as scientific 'food' should be carefully sniffed and tasted prior to swallowing.

In 2017, more measurable studies were conducted at both Stanford and Mexico City universities. These studies revealed the current rate of vertebrate extinction during the twentieth century was two species per year.[56] This information provided a factual basis for some degree of concern.

---

[55] William Reville, Irish Times, Dec 8, 2016

[56] The Irish News, 11 July, 2017

Prophets Of Secular Society

How things change! How many cartoons have been drawn through the ages where religious people were portrayed carrying signs saying, "The end is nigh?" It now appears that religious doom-sayers have largely been replaced by doomsayers from the science community.

Clearly identifying himself as an atheist, Stephen Hawking likened people who believe there is life after death to children who are afraid of the dark. It was one area where the great man was out of his depth. If he had observed someone in an authentic relationship with the Almighty, he would have seen a person so busy having a love affair with the Light that the darkness wasn't even a consideration. Not to be disrespectful though, all it did was prove his humanity. Hawking was thought by many to be the brightest scientific mind since Einstein.

On the other side of the atheistic coin, thousands of Bible commentators show that the Bible has a vastly different and more hopeful description regarding the future of mankind.[57] The prophets of secular society would happily make the Church an extinct body and lay it to rest alongside the Tasmanian Tiger (1936) and the Desert Bandicoot (1943). Though it will never happen, it does beg the following question:

---

[57] Matthew 25:31–33

Will There Be A Church On Future Earth?

Worshippers are a gregarious lot and tend to do life in groups. A group of cattle is called a herd, a group of owls is called a parliament and a group of worshippers is called a Church.

As much bad press as the Church has been given and often deserves, the whole world will always need the authenticity, honesty and hope of its message. It has been a confusion to society that the Church down through the ages has an ability to both sin spectacularly and then use up yet another of God's endless supply of second chances. Justice demands that the Church should have been hung, drawn and quartered on many occasions. Thankfully, it does not survive on justice. Hollywood action movies do and so does every court of law. On occasions, humanity would love God to be as angry with the Church as He was with Sodom and Gomorrah. His displeasure gave those two sin-cities a serious belting.[58] It is because of grace that He won't. He extends an almost endless supply of grace and loudly declares that where sin abounds, grace abounds more.[59]

We humans are a strange and predictable lot. Often, we want God to mete out His justice to those who get under our skin, whilst asking Him for one more dose of forgiveness for ourselves; another chance to do things better.

---

[58] Genesis 19

[59] Romans 5:20

One reason why the Church will not fade into oblivion is because God keeps reviving it. It can be likened to a gardener taking a cutting from a plant that once bore beautiful fruit. He discards the old and plants the new for a fresh new beginning.

The Church simply will not go away despite hostile campaigns and predictions to that effect in almost every preceding generation. Voltaire, Friedrich Nietzsche and Bertrand Russell all predicted the end of Christianity and faith. In the 2020s, the charge is being led by people like Sam Harris, a graduate in philosophy from Stanford University. He keeps battering at the walls of religious faith, especially that of Christianity and Islam. His first book, The End of Faith (2004), was a New York Times bestseller.[60]

In the 18th century, Voltaire famously predicted that Christianity would be extinct within 100 years of his death. Ironically, his estate became a Bible Society headquarters that went on to print multiple thousands of Bibles for a hungry worldwide audience.

Dying in 1976, Chairman Mao thought he had exterminated Christianity. If Mao could have seen China in 2020, he would have had a conniption. Whilst officially an atheist nation, the Church is multiplying in China at an amazing rate. "By my calculations, China is destined to become the largest Christian country in the world very soon," said Fenggang Yang, a professor of sociology at

---

[60] "Atheist Apostle," David Aikman, Christianity Today, March 5, 2007

Purdue University and author of 'Religion in China: Survival and Revival under Communist Rule'. He believed that the number of Christians would swell to around 160 million by 2025, putting China ahead of the United States.[61]

Here is the point. The Church could be led by people wearing 15th century robes and caps, or tee shirts and jeans with holes in them. It could meet in centuries-old cathedrals, modern convention centres or on-line. Its services could go for 45 minutes or one and a half hours. It could be found in a communist nation or free, but all that has to happen for the Church to find its way forward is for God to speak to someone with a listening ear; someone who will be deeply impacted. That person will put whatever they were doing on hold and hive off in a bold new direction, empowered by the love of God.

People like Martin Luther and William Tyndale were God's ideas in the 1400s and 1500s. In the 1400s, a German goldsmith by the name of Johannes Gutenberg, invented a printing press that could print the written word at breakneck speed. The fastest of scribes could not have produced in one year the number of copies of the New Testament that a Gutenberg-like press could produce in just a few weeks.[62]

In the 16th Century, reformation spread across Europe and Tyndale's Bible was illegally printed and smuggled to

---

[61] Tom Phillips, Liushi, Zhejiang province 19 Apr 2014, The Telegraph

[62] What Tyndale Owed Gutenberg, Raymond A. Lajoie, Christian History Magazine

its hungry readers in many nations. He was in a hurry, because he knew that this activity would cost him his life.

On Oct 6,1536, at the approximate age of 42, he was taken from his cell at Castle Vilvoorden in Belgium to be publicly executed. His last words before being strangled and burnt at the stake were, "Lord, open the King of England's eyes."

Had Henry VIII been in Belgium at the time, he would have happily strangled him with his own royal hands. Tyndale previously objected to the annulment of Henry's marriage and Henry had angrily snapped. Two years later, the same Henry tilted his crown in the opposite direction and authorised the Great Bible for the Church of England which was drawn largely from Tyndale's work.

In every century, the Church has been revived and found its way forward. If it can survive the persecution and turbulence of the 16th Century, one might conclude it can survive anything. Some predict extinction, but history declares the opposite.

HOW MUCH TIME DO WE HAVE THIS SIDE OF THE GRAVE?

Australia's Oldest Person

How much time? More than we initially thought.

When Miriam Schmierer (1899–2011) passed away she was aged 112 and the oldest recorded person in Australia. In 1901, she was two years old at the time Edmund Barton became Australia's first prime minister. She continued living through the terms of another 26. She and her husband Grenville worked their dairy farm for many years in the beautiful North Burnett region in Queensland. Widowed in 1965, she had no idea she had so many years yet to live. At 91, Miriam decided it was time to admit herself to Masters Lodge, a nursing home in Hervey Bay, Queensland. She approached this new season of her life with a deep sense of mission. It seemed to her that everyone around her was on death row. Looking around at the inmates, she would have considered them a pretty tough congregation.

As time went by, she became aware of an inescapable fact. She would say, "I feel like I'm in God's waiting room and people keep going in before me."

How much time do we have this side of the grave? Miriam had eons more than she imagined and today, a lengthening average life span is presenting individuals and governments with a raft of complications.

The Complications Of Ageing

The Commonwealth of Australia federated its six States under a written constitution on January 1, 1901. Between 1908 and 1910, laws were passed whereby males could receive an old age pension at age 65 and females at 60. The average life expectancy in 1908? 58 years of age.

In other words, if someone got lucky and beat the average by seven years, they would receive a small pension to tide them over until their funeral.

In 2019, approximately 85 countries provided an old age pension of some sort. An article in The Guardian[63] in 2015 identified the top countries to grow old in. At the top of the list was that 'little bewdy' (beauty) Australia, followed by Germany, Japan and the Nordic countries.

In Australia, the average life expectancy in 2018 for baby boomers had risen. In 2020, it was around 84 and going north. The nation's thriving medical industry continues to provide its fair share of headaches for politicians who are trying to manage a budget that has by necessity a very heavy financial burden for the elderly and aging.

The World Health Organisation (W.H.O.) agrees entirely. "The world is facing a situation without precedent. We soon will have more older people than children and more

---

[63] The Guardian, Helen Davidson, Kate Connolly, Justin McCurry, David Crouch, Shaun Walker, Mary O'Hara, David Smith, Stephanie Kirchgaessner, Anne Penketh, Henry McDonald Wed 4 Mar 2015

people at extreme old age than ever before. As both the proportion of older people and the length of life increase throughout the world, key questions arise. Will population aging be accompanied by a longer period of good health, a sustained sense of well-being and extended periods of social engagement and productivity, or will it be associated with more illness, disability, and dependency?"

"In 2010, an estimated 524 million people were aged 65 or older – eight percent of the world's population. By 2050, this number is expected to nearly triple to about 1.5 billion, representing 16% of the world's population."

"The global number of centenarians is projected to increase 10-fold between 2010 and 2050. In the mid 1990s, some researchers estimated that, over the course of human history, the odds of living from birth to age 100 may have risen from 1 in 20,000,000 to 1 in 50 for females in low mortality nations such as Japan and Sweden."[64]

In 2018, the WHO speculated that our age brackets may have to be redefined for the future in the following ways:

- 0-17 years old: Underage
- 18-65 years old: Youth/young people
- 66-79 years old: Middle-aged
- 80-99 years old: Elderly/senior
- 100+ years old: Long-lived/elderly[65]

---

[64] Global Health and Aging (PDF), www.who.int/ageing/publications/global_health.pdf

[65] Victoria Tunggono for Brilio English, Jan 20, 2016

Who could argue with this? Certainly not Yuichiro Miura, an 80-year-old Japanese man who had four heart operations before becoming the oldest person to climb the 8,850 metre peak of Mount Everest in 2013. The following week[66] an 81-year-old Nepalese man who held the previous record, planned another ascent. Min Bahadur Sherchan failed on that occasion, but undeterred, he made another attempt at age 85. He made it to base camp where sadly, he suffered a fatal heart attack.

In the Australian 2016 Census of population and housing, the Australian Bureau of Statistics recorded 2,897 students aged 80 years and over. Since then, 60 to 75-year-olds began repeating a scenario like the one below.

Hypothetical Albert and hypothetical Doris hypothetically retired when he turned 65. Armed with a gold watch for his 45 years of faithful service and an inadequate amount of superannuation, they bought a four-wheel drive and a caravan and headed out on the grey nomad trail. 12 years of increasing monotony passed and by now, they were rediscovering the same trails and running into familiar faces. Hypothetical Albert noticed he and Doris were not decaying as quickly as they expected. "Dorrie," he asked one day, "what about we go back to studying? After all, our minds are still active and healthy, even if our bodies aren't as mobile as they used to be."

---

[66] The Weekend Australian, May 23, 2013

The Increase In Life Expectancy

There is a smallish office in London's Whitehall called the Department for Work and Pensions. It is tradition in the United Kingdom and British Commonwealth for the reigning Monarch to send congratulatory telegrams to those who are still batting on bravely at 100 not out.[67] Queen Elizabeth herself is no spring chicken. Her Majesty turned 95 on April 21, 2021.

Though little-known, the office has a staff that has steadily been growing in number. In 2014, it had a seven-strong 'Centenarian team' dedicated to keeping information on Britain's oldest citizens up to date. Their statistics revealed that the number of people over the age of 100 had jumped by 70 per cent in a decade.[68] Estimates published by the Office of National Statistics (ONS) showed that there were almost 14,000 people over the age of 100 living in the UK. This figure was about to explode with the ONS estimating that there were 527,240 people over the age of 90 in the UK in 2013. This accounted for over one per cent of the entire population. To add to this, the number of people aged over 105 almost doubled from 360 in 2003 to 710 in 2013.

People started getting the idea that the baby 'boom' at the completion of World War II (1945) was actually more of a

---

[67] "A century is a score of 100 or more runs in a single innings." (Wikipedia)

[68] John Bingham, Social Affairs Editor, The Telegraph, 25 Sep 2014

'kaboom!' As time went by, the Centenarian Staff were reduced and artificially intelligent assistants now send the telegrams on Her Majesty's behalf.

The World's Blue Zones

The phenomenon of worldwide increase in life expectancy has inspired a flurry of intellectual activity. Gerontologists, demographers and professors in biometry are now going full tilt in this area of research. It became common language in this field of research to refer to those pockets of planet earth where communities of long livers were found as 'Blue Zones'. Why Blue Zones? Because Dr Michel Poulain, a Belgian researcher studying the unusually high concentration of centenarians in the Barbagia region on the Island of Sardinia, circled the relevant area with a blue pen.[69]

In America, the National Institute boasted the presence of a pre-eminent researcher, Dr Robert Kane, who helped shape the Blue Zones premise. The Sam and Ann Barshop Centre for Longevity and Aging in Texas enlarged its activity and reputation. Additionally, the (NARI) in Australia popped up, together with the National Institute on Ageing (NIA) at Ryersone University in Canada. Centres of research in Europe and the Netherlands, plus many more, exemplified the importance of this thing that was happening around planet earth.

There are a number of confirmed longevity hotspots, or Blue Zones. As well as the Barbagia region in Sardinia, Okinawans in Japan managed to reach the age of 100 at

---

[69] P27, The Blue Zones, Second Edition, Dan Buettner, Pub; National Geographic

a rate three times higher than Americans. Nicoya Peninsula in Costa Rica, the Greek Island of Ikaria and the community of Loma Linda in California were others.

And the conclusion of all this research? How will it benefit the human race? The consensus was that if the secrets of longevity from these Blue Zones could be captured, another ten years could be added to a person's life span before their appointment with the undertaker. To make it clear, if a person would have died at 92, the harnessing of these secrets could extend their life until 102. For many, this finding did not inspire geriatric cartwheels. So, why have so many in academic circles expressed excitement about these findings?

Thirsting For The Fountain Of Youth

Maybe their interest does not just go back to academic roots. Maybe there was another force at play that should be considered. For centuries, people groups mythologised about a spring of water commonly referred to as the fountain of youth. Writings in the 5th Century BC mentioned this spring of water and it was brought to life again in the 'Alexander Romance' (3rd Century AD), a series of legends concerning the mythical exploits of Alexander the Great. When the Spanish explorer Juan Ponce De Leon landed on the northeast corner of Florida on April 2,1513, it was rumoured he was searching for the same waterhole. It wasn't true, but the legend stuck.

Over the centuries, this spring of water with magical powers evolved into a wonder pill, a breakthrough diet or a new medical procedure. There isn't much the human race has not tried in an effort to delay the aging process. Transfiguring ourselves with surgery until our skin provides no more elasticity to play with, we poor darlings have become the modern-day reminders of the futility of searching for this elusive billabong. But ... in the face of this, planet earth had, and still has, a spiritual and philosophical dilemma. In the midst of all scientific research and mythological quackery, mankind has an internal, unshakeable belief that we are eternal beings.

One would think that by now the earth would have become a far less religious planet than it is; that media fervour and scientific skepticism should have convinced people that faith in a living God is an outdated concept; that there is no such person as God and that once you're dead, you're dead. Finito. No more. End of story. Nothing follows.

HOW MUCH TIME DO WE HAVE THE OTHER SIDE OF THE GRAVE?

What Most People Believe

Where does the term 'Pandora's box' come from? It was an artifact in Greek mythology that when opened, led to 'any amount of great and unexpected troubles.'[70]

Any discussion about life after death can open this box. Sometimes it is an exciting, rewarding conversation. Other times it can be characterised by dispute and anger.

In 2017, Pew Research Centre asserted that about 80-85% of the earth's global 7.3 billion residents identified themselves as religious.[71] All religions have definite beliefs about eternity. Therefore, we must ask; why, why, why does the global community continue believing in life after death? The book of Ecclesiastes provides the answer. "He has planted (an awareness) of eternity in the human heart."[72]

This immoveable seed of 'knowing' has been planted and resides within each person. When all the noise and arguments die down, there it is, quecela nous plaise ou non.[73] Mankind has been unable to shake off this knowledge; this quiet nagging; even if it is no more than an inkling that suggests there is something more.

At one end of the faith spectrum is the aggressive critic of

---

[70] Chambers Dictionary, 1998

[71] Pew Research Centre Factank, April 5th, 2017

[72] Ecclesiastes 3:11

[73] "Whether you like it or not"

all things spiritual. This is the one who has no more belief that there could be life beyond a terminal heart attack other than the tiniest piece of uncertainty that perhaps they could be wrong. At the other end of the spectrum are the totally convinced who display an assured belief in eternal life based on the claim that they have met, and continue to meet with, the Living God. These would assert that failing to consider their mortality against the backdrop of eternity is akin to looking at the moon and failing to see that its light is a reflection of something greater.

So, for one, extra years of life in the flesh indicate great scientific and medical advancement. For the other, those additional years would weigh much lighter when compared against life that goes on for eternity.

The Mystery Of Aging

In his book titled 'The Blue Zones', Dan Buettner states, "The brutal reality about aging is that it only has an accelerator pedal. We have yet to discover whether a brake exists for people. The name of the game is to keep from pushing the accelerator pedal so hard that we speed up the aging process."[74] But according to the Bible, ageing was something earth's first inhabitants did not experience.

The most beautiful garden in the world, the 32-hectare Keukenhof flower garden in Lisse (Western Netherlands), would have faded in comparison to the garden that earth's first occupants enjoyed.

This couple had carte blanch to enjoy everything in the garden; well, almost. Clearly informed that they were not to eat the fruit from one particular tree, one could only imagine the conversation between God and his two kids as he was evicting them from the garden.

"One thing! You only had to remember one thing!"

In one act of madness with centuries of consequences, Adam and Eve incurred the death penalty for the whole human race. "If you eat its fruit, you are sure to die."[75] They had been warned, and people have been aging (and dying) ever since.

---

[74] P4 The Blue Zones, Second Edition, Dan Buettner, Pub; National Geographic
[75] Genesis 2:17 NLT

Hopeful Voices

For those who have little fear of death and an exciting confidence that eternity follows on, the bonus of a couple of extra decades of life is viewed very differently to those trying to hang onto their mortality for as long as possible. Many in the scientific community spanning many generations have argued that science is not antagonistic towards faith-based thinking.

Isaac Newton said, "Gravity explains the motions of the planets, but it cannot explain who set the planets in motion. God governs all things and knows all that is or can be done."[76]

Johannes Kepler developed many ideas about the laws of planetary motion. He believed in a brilliant creator.

Other highly intelligent people like Englishman Henry Thornton, a close relative and friend of William Wilberforce, was motivated by a passionate faith in God. Thornton is considered to be the father of central banking. Wilberforce was a politician and well known Christian spokesperson of a radical and highly influential people group in the late 1770s and early 1800s. They were known in their day as the Clapham Group and were responsible for abolishing slavery and improving the quality of life in England and its colonies. So influential were they that it was said that the ethos of the Clapham

---

[76] Tyler Huckabee for RELEVANT Media Group, April 11, 2014

Group became the spirit of the age. What motivated them? Was it blind faith, or a sense of purpose that sprang from a considered study of Jesus Christ and His resurrection? Were they just a superstitious community? Was their faith inherited or inherent?

Whilst Christians are expected to back up their faith in Christ with sound logic and evidence after a born-again experience, very few new believers do exhaustive research prior to this 'birth'. For most, they are compelled by a mysterious power to open up and receive Him. This is followed in many cases by years of working out what on earth just happened. God is never surprised by all the questions thrown at Him. He has been answering the same ones for multiple millennia.

Serious Research Into The Validity Of Faith-Based Living

Of course, if someone came back to life after their death and started acting eternally, we would have evidence to support a belief regarding eternity. Has that happened?

Did Jesus Christ actually die and come back to life? When we pray, are we talking to an actual person who lived in human form about 2,000 years ago? Or, are we speaking to a romantic notion? Is He really still alive and communicating from a realm of existence just beyond our physical senses? Are mortal residents on planet earth in the process of becoming immortal residents in eternity?

A mountain of research has been conducted over many centuries examining actual evidence for the resurrection of Jesus Christ. This research is essential and vital if we are to answer the question, "How much time do we have the other side of the grave?"

Simon Greenleaf - Harvard Law School

One such researcher was Simon Greenleaf (December 5, 1783–October 6,1853). Greenleaf came to be regarded as a legal genius and is worthy of interest.

In 1806, Simon Greenleaf began practising law in New Gloucester, Massachusetts. This was exactly the same time Wilberforce and company in England were in a pitch battle for the abolishment of slavery. Years ahead in 1833, his stellar career led him to partner with Professor Joseph Story at Harvard Law School. Anyone who graduates from Harvard today, comes to any employer with significant distinction. However, in 1833 things were much different. Greenleaf arrived in its less than hallowed halls to prop up a seriously sick institution. Only four years earlier, Harvard was about to enter its third decade with only six students.

If it were not for both Nathan Dane (Harvard's generous benefactor) and Josiah Quincy (its new president), there may not have been a Harvard for Greenleaf to come to. In the fall of 1833, things were improving and Harvard boasted a record number of 56 enrolled students. With that humble beginning, Greenleaf helped put Harvard Law School on the academic map. He received the title of Royal Professor at Law in 1834 and in due course, was also awarded the Honorary Doctor of Laws degree by Harvard, Amherst and the University of Alabama.

In 1842, Simon Greenleaf published the first volume of his

masterwork titled 'A Treatise on the Law of Evidence' (3 vols. 1842–1853). This work has been described as 'the greatest single authority in the entire literature of legal procedure'.[77] In layman's terms, Greenleaf made this monumental contribution to the U.S. legal system by setting out the rules and principles for gathering evidence and conducting cross-examination; rules and principles still relied on today by the U.S. judicial system.

As a legal scholar, Greenleaf wondered if Jesus' resurrection would meet his stringent tests for gathering evidence. He wondered whether or not the evidence for it would hold up in a court of law. Focusing his brilliant legal mind on the facts of history, Greenleaf began applying his rules of evidence to the case of Jesus' resurrection and began examining the witnesses of the crucifixion and resurrection of Christ.

As their testimonies were assessed, contrary to what skeptics might have expected, the more Greenleaf investigated the record of history, the more evidence he discovered that supported the claim that Jesus had indeed risen from the tomb.[78]

So, what was that evidence? Greenleaf observed several dramatic changes that took place shortly after Jesus died. The most baffling being the behaviour of the disciples. It wasn't just one or two disciples who

---

[77] Knott, The Dictionary of American Biography, back cover of The Testimony of the Evangelists

[78] Y–Jesus; The facts about Jesus Presented by Scholars 2018

insisted Jesus had risen. It was all of them. Applying his own rules of evidence to the facts, Greenleaf arrived at his verdict.

He accepted Jesus' resurrection as the best explanation for the events that took place immediately after his crucifixion. To this brilliant legal scholar, it would have been impossible for the disciples to persist with their conviction that Jesus had risen if they hadn't actually seen Him.[79] From there, Greenleaf would go on to write the 3 volumes of 'The Testimony of the Evangelists' and gain recognition as a prominent 19th Century Christian apologist. Greenleaf used his findings to defend and explain Christianity in his writings.

History tells us that these same disciples (excluding John) met brutal deaths. For these ones to maintain their testimony throughout their entire lives, even in the face of torture and death, strengthened Greenleaf's conclusion. After all, why lay down your life for a lie?

Was Greenleaf's voice an isolated one?

Not for a moment. Sir Lionel Luckhoo (1914–1997) is considered one of the greatest lawyers in British history. He is recorded in the Guinness Book of World Records as the 'World's Most Successful Advocate' with 245 consecutive murder acquittals. He also applied his legal mind to the case for the resurrection of Christ. In his later years, he stated:

---

[79] Simon Greenleaf, 1874, The Testimony of the Evangelists. New York, NY: 28

"I humbly add I have spent more than 42 years as a defence trial lawyer appearing in many parts of the world and am still in active practice. I have been fortunate to secure a number of successes in jury trials and I say unequivocally the evidence for the Resurrection of Jesus Christ is so overwhelming that it compels acceptance by proof which leaves absolutely no room for doubt."[80]

---

[80] Sir Lionel Luckhoo, The Question Answered: Did Jesus Rise from the Dead? Luckhoo Booklets, back page.
http://www.hawaiichristiansonline.com/sir_lionel.html.

Frank Morrison - 'Who Moved The Stone?'

Many others have conducted their own research. One of these very interesting personalities was Frank Morison. Over the years, he was variously described as a rationalistic lawyer, an engineer and an atheist. He was none of these. In fact, he wasn't even Frank Morison! Albert Henry Ross (1881–1950) used Frank Morison as a pseudonym. An advertising agent and a freelance writer, he described himself as a journalist. Due to the thoroughness of his research and the brilliance of his findings, it was assumed that he held many more academic qualifications than he actually did.

He was in fact an unusual skeptic. Unusual in that he was attracted to and liked the biblical Jesus. However, he was persuaded miracles did not happen, especially ones of resurrectional magnitude. Yet, he was drawn to Jesus as a moth is drawn to a flame. He put his keen mind to work in order to untangle the cobweb of stories being told within many historical documents. Ross pressed forward to prove, once and for all, that a dead man would not come back to life.

He did not just study the Gospels. He looked beyond them to other sources, such as the works of Josephus, some early historical writings on Pontius Pilate and other relevant source material. As Ross advanced through his work, he began writing a book he had initially intended to publish under the title 'Jesus: The Last Phase'. It was to deal with the last seven days of Jesus' life on earth. As he continued his research, the evidence that Jesus did indeed rise from his tomb, became more and more convincing. Everything pointed to it. The book he set out to write that debunked the risen Christ, was not the book he completed. He renamed it 'Who Moved the Stone?' In the chapter 'The Book That Refused to be Written', he plainly states that the book he intended to write in one way finished in another. He was brought to, as he calls it, the 'unexpected shores of salvation'.[81]

Originally published in 1944, his book has been reprinted a whopping nine times. The latest reprint occurred in 2006.

Here is the point. If Jesus Christ rose from the dead, He proved that life between birth and death was merely the first instalment of a life that continues beyond death.

Let us leave the final words on this matter to Professor Greenleaf.

"Either the men of Galilee were men of superlative wisdom, and extensive knowledge and experience, and of deeper skill in the arts of deception than any and all others, before them or after them, or they have truly stated astonishing things which they saw and heard."

"A person who rejects Christ may choose to say they do not accept it (His resurrection), but they cannot choose to say there is not enough evidence."

---

[81] The Times. 1950. Mr. A. H. Ross (Obituaries). p.8; Morison, F. 2006 (most recent edition). Who moved the stone?

"According to the laws of legal evidence used in courts of law, there is more evidence for the historical fact of the resurrection of Jesus Christ than for just about any other event in history."

"Of the Divine character of the Bible, I think, no man who deals honestly with his own mind and heart can entertain a reasonable doubt. For myself, I must say, that having for many years made the evidences of Christianity the subject of close study, the result has been a firm and increasing conviction of the authenticity and plenary inspiration of the Bible. It is indeed the Word of God."[82]

---

[82] Is Simon Greenleaf Still Relevant? By Robert R. Edwards, B.A., B.S., J.D. Famous Quotes Regarding the Evidence for The Resurrection of Jesus, Evidence for Christianity, Aug 10th, 2008 http://www.azquotes.com/author/4...

SMILING AT THE FUTURE

A Lady Called Wisdom

The Book of Proverbs is the story of two ladies, both vying for our affection. Its purpose is to help us smile when we consider the future. Without a biblical perspective, it is easy to be apprehensive, even anxious, as we contemplate the future through the filter of the past. The Book of Proverbs in the Bible is often referred to as the Book of Wisdom. Wisdom is amazing stuff. It sees into things. It adds things up. It takes complicated things and makes them simple and then finds a way to apply them to the way we live. There are so many ways to look into the future but the only correct way will be through the filter of wisdom.

Cultivating wisdom is so important! Let us spend the final moments of this book enriching our lives with it. Let's go.

In all 31 chapters of the Book of Proverbs, wisdom is referred to as 'She'. Whilst there is a cast of colourful characters throughout the Proverbs, we have to wait until the very final Proverb to go backstage and meet the leading lady. When we do, we discover how content and settled a person can be when they have learned the many lessons wisdom wants us to learn in the preceding proverbs.

Her completion is our potential.

All of the main characters throughout the Proverbs are real and all of them are metaphors for someone else.

First, we are introduced to a father.[83] The real father is Solomon and he is a metaphor for Father God. Then, there is a son who is naïve; as clueless as any teenager about to collide with the unforeseen challenges, opportunities and possible pitfalls of adulthood. The real son, we could safely guess, is one of Solomon's eldest or favourite children. He is also a metaphor for all of us. Solomon probably began fatherhood with great enthusiasm and commitment, but as time went by, he began accumulating wives in the same way a fully absorbed numismatist collects coins.[84] He progressively went downhill in his later years and was unable to heed his own advice for the full duration of his life.

Moving on, we are introduced to 'enticing sinners'.[85] The world is still full of shabby, unscrupulous characters ready to take advantage of the unsuspecting, ready to catch us in our naivety.

---

[83] Proverbs 1:8

[84] 1 Kings 11:1–3

[85] Proverbs 1:10

Meet Prudence

We could name the woman in Proverbs 31, 'Prudence.' Apart from being the embodiment of wisdom, she is a passionate, plain talking, definite kind of girl. She is also a metaphor for Jesus Christ 'in whom lie hidden all the treasures of wisdom and knowledge'.[86] Although, she is not without competition.

In the ninth Proverb, we are introduced to another girl. This young lady is a brash, purposeless individual who goes by the name of 'Folly'. These two ladies battle for our affections all of our lives.

Amongst the generous cast of supporting actors, we find a promiscuous woman who has unknowingly decided to make life considerably worse for herself by abandoning her husband in favour of sex without love. There is a viticulturist cum grain producer, who honours God with the first and best of his produce, and whose barns and vats overflow with the smell of success. There is another immoral woman who has very high gloss and very cheap merchandise. She has an endless set of descending stairs for those foolish enough to go through her front door. We find a naïve, inexperienced young man personally guaranteeing another man's debt, whilst risking his own financial security and closest relationships. And, what unfolding drama would be complete without a person

---

[86] Colossians 2:3

with the motivation of a sloth on Phenergan being exhorted to stare at an ant community until he sees the folly of his laziness?

[87] In the midst of them all stands 'Pru.' She has found something to stand on beside the thoroughfare of life and through her tears she pleads with everyone to listen to her message. This remarkable lady lives her life in the present with the future as a backdrop. She encourages us to do the same.

Prudence is a special kind of wisdom that considers the future.

Her lessons teach us to be sexually moral, humble, financially smart and honest, gracious with our words, hardworking and far sighted. She teaches us to be strategic with our planning skills and aware that alcohol has the power to distort our good judgement; that we should be self-controlled rather than hot tempered, live life optimistically rather than fearfully, be friendly, and orchestrate a life-long learning curve with respect for our elders. She encourages us to build the type of reputation that makes it difficult for our critics to find serious flaws.

We find the sum total of all the preceding Proverbs in the final one. If all this wisdom were to be gathered together in one person, it would look like this amazing woman. When we get up close and personal, we find that her wisdom is found in the practical expressions of her faith.

---

[87] Proverbs 9:3–6

No doubt her commitment to her local Church and her enthusiasm in worship were huge foundational influences in her life, but none of this is mentioned in Proverbs 31. No, it concentrates on how she was inspired to live out her faith every day of the week for the betterment of others.

How Did She Become Wise?

One strong possibility is that she would have taken her own advice and purchased it. [88]Paying for knowledge and wisdom is no new concept. These have been commercial commodities for centuries. Accumulating opinions and ideas from others is a poor substitute.

Pru's urgent advice to us all is to buy the truth, buy wisdom and never sell it. She urges us to make a profit in our lives by exchanging something of value for this thing of far greater value.

Her first quality is that she is an 'excellent wife'[89] whose worth is 'above jewels'. The largest and most painful battlefield across the world is the home. Behind front doors, disputes, deception, domestic violence and a host of other erosive values are driving people from the relationships they previously expected would be nurturing and safe. Our Proverbs 31 woman must have been a committed student of relationships; especially that of the marriage covenant.

There is a **second quality** that flows on from the first. Her children 'rise up and bless her'. [90]Her husband knows she is not going to play up behind his back when he is away on official business. She has made an art form of bringing

---

[88] Proverbs 23:23

[89] Proverbs 31:10

[90] Proverbs 31:28

value into their marriage and family on a daily basis. Her children think they are the most fortunate kids in the playground. In every family, children are born before the wisdom necessary to raise them has been learned. Pru must have been an intuitive and committed learner of motherhood and parenting.

When did she discover she was **clever with her hands**? Whenever it happened, she not only discovered what she was good at, but she also developed a **business acumen** that turned her hobbies and interests into income streams. Starting at home, she began spinning yarns and threads for the sought-after fashion industry of her day. Before long, she was exporting fabrics and importing food.

One thing we know: this girl **knew how to work**! A true vision is one that will inspire us to do ridiculously amazing things with our time. She was up before dawn, and sometimes she burned midnight oil, but she **planned her time well** because no business responsibilities robbed her of spending time with her happy and well-fed family. Added to this were her **real estate conquests**.

She had **perspective**. Rather than concentrating on becoming the richest person in town, she knew that there would always be **those less fortunate**. She had a heart for them and she helped them. Her not-for-profit activities continually kept her soft-hearted and authentic. She specialised in bed-spreads. Cold Israeli nights needed warmth and comfort, and more than once she would have noticed these bedspreads wrapped around those sleeping rough. She was equally comfortable visiting the digs of the poor and the palaces of the rich and influential. A girl that knew how to turn heads when she entered a room, her fine linen and purple gowns would have been featured in Jerusalem's top fashion publications.

Pru listened more than she spoke, but when she did speak, rooms would have fallen silent. Her words bore the mark of a lifetime spent pondering how to use the powerful tool of well-chosen phrases to bless and build others. No one could remember the last time she used sarcasm in her conversation. She was **continually learning** and growing in her quest to be a committed lifelong learner.

And, that smile. What was that smile? When the room emptied and people headed for home, the memory of that smile went with them. On occasions, the observer twigged. It was a smile that looked at the future with confidence. She had her life, her marriage, her family, her friends, her business activities and her plans for the future all humming along nicely. She was busy, balanced and content. Pru, like all of us, knew she would one day die ready for an eternity with her number one love. However, this event would not occur before she had lived her life on earth to the full.

THE ONLY CONCLUSION THAT MATTERS

Up To You

As a young thirty-something year-old, I asked a wise person, "what's to become of me?"

"Well David," my friend answered, "that is up to you."

That snippet of truth applies to all of us.

Thank you for sticking with me as I have tried to provide a glimpse of the future. We are in the midst of amazing times where the technology revolution has brought to us a literal world of information that can be accessed at the speed of now. We have looked at the creative side of mankind and flipped the coin over to look at the corrupt side. In 2021, we are emerging from a global plague, although not all of us.

We have tackled questions regarding longevity and eternity, asking how much time we have on both this side and the other side of the grave.

Finally, we met a lady called wisdom who has insights that are without parallel and that offer us help and encouragement for our own lives.

All that remains is to draw our conclusions and consider our way forwards.

When a person contemplates the future and considers what they should do in preparation, conclusions are drawn and choices about how to live are made. Whatever conclusions are drawn, the only ones that ultimately matter are our own. Whilst God has a marvelous plan for our lives, he has placed our hands on the steering wheel, and the direction we take is of our own choosing.

When formulating our conclusions, we owe it to ourselves to remove anything that could bias our thinking. Many people disagree with the notion that God could be real and that life goes on forever, because the message-carriers have behaved badly. It is true that we humans inflict great pain on each other, and pain from those we thought we could trust is always the worst kind. Unfortunately, while pain is a great reminder, it can be a poor teacher.

My personal conclusion is that everyone survives death and lives forever. There is no proof that we don't and compelling evidence that we do. Consequently, I and people like me, have chosen biblical values to live by and have diligently prepared for what lies ahead. David Gelernter, Professor of Computer Science at Yale University, would struggle to agree with me. He is still traveling along his great journey of contemplation.

He gives us an indication of this in his essay titled 'Giving up Darwin – A fond farewell to a brilliant and beautiful theory'. However, in farewelling Charles Darwin's theory of evolution, Gelernter does not automatically swing the pendulum to the opposite side where he falls into the arms of a loving Saviour.

His questions and comments appear to be without bias and represent a learned scientist's quest for truth.

Needless to say, that should inspire us to do the same. He writes:[91]

"Like so many others, I grew up with Darwin's theory and had always believed it was true. I had heard doubts over the years from well-informed and sometimes brilliant people, but I had my hands full cultivating my garden, and it was easier to let biology take care of itself. But, in recent years, reading and discussion have shut that road down for good.

This is sad. It is no victory of any sort for religion. It is a defeat for human ingenuity. It means one less beautiful idea in our world, and one more hugely difficult and important problem back on mankind's to-do list. But, we each need to make our peace with the facts and not try to make life on earth simpler than it really is."

He goes on to say:

"There's no reason to doubt that Darwin successfully explained the small adjustments by which an organism adapts to local circumstances: changes to fur, density or wing style or beak shape. Yet there are many reasons to doubt whether he can answer the hard questions and explain the big picture—not the fine-tuning of existing species but the emergence of new ones. The origin of species is exactly what Darwin **cannot** explain."

In questioning the role of God in creation, he asks:

"If there was an intelligent designer, what was his strategy?

---

[91] Claremont Review of Books, Spring 2019, Giving up Darwin, David Gelernter

How did He manage to back Himself into so many corners, wasting energy on so many doomed organisms? What was His purpose? And why did He do such a slipshod job? Why are we so disease-prone, heart broke-prone and so on?"

In the documentary interview 'Uncommon Knowledge with Peter Robinson', a production of the Hoover Institution,[92] Gelernter plays the devil's advocate and attacks the problem from a creationist point of view.

"When we ask the question is it good that the earth was created? Is it good that the universe was created? Is it good that it happened? Many people agree that it is not good, that it is a catastrophe. If we had to go back and do it all again, we would have to tell the Almighty "Don't do it! The suffering outweighs the good."

He continues, "God's creation was good, but almost as soon as man was made, he commenced screwing life up. They began arguing, struggling and being a nuisance in every conceivable way. So, God creates a perfect world ... on the other hand He doesn't create a perfect creature. Mankind is a bitch."

Our fascinating Professor scores physical creation as a nine out of ten and human creation as a one out of ten. There is an obvious logic to his concerns. Planet earth does not have good and bad people. If that were the case, we could attempt the futile exercise of separating the two

---

[92] https://www.youtube.com/watch?v=noj4phMT9OE

groups. No. We have people in every nation who are both good and bad. Creative and corrupt.

Like so many others, he begins his investigation at the end in an attempt to find the beginning. He is disappointed with the end result and cannot yet fathom the cause. There is no doubt that Professor Gelernter would quickly unearth the reason for the corrupt nature of mankind, his greatest disappointment, by reading a chronological version of the Bible with an enquiring mind. He could well meet Lady Wisdom on the way.

In the preceding pages, I have endeavoured to inspire an exciting and rewarding contemplation. Perhaps, even offering a fresh look at the age-old questions regarding mankind's existence, purpose and future.

Our creative nature gives us a clue to who we are.

Our corrupt nature gives us a clue to what has happened to us.

Our conclusions need to be accurate and made without bias.

My hope is that in the busyness of life, you will put the lesser things aside and make time to find the answers that help you smile at the future.

RESOURCES BY DAVID SCHAEFFER

- Grieve Upwards – One Man's Journey Through the Valley
- Stress Less Live More – Everyday Stress, Everyday Solutions
- Smile at the Future – Finding Hope That Lasts a Lifetime
- Charge at the Dark – Unleashing Courage That Lasts a Lifetime
- The Home Improvements Manual – Building families That Last a Lifetime

They can be purchased through his website, www.davidschaeffer.com.au or through most on-line book distributors.

David is an experienced and qualified coach/mentor. He facilitates a life design program, *Design a Decade* (www.designadecade.com) and also provides coaching/mentoring in the following areas.

- Self-leadership
- Recovery from Loss
- Stress Minimization
- Self-awareness
- Building Quality Relationships
- Church leadership

Contact David at: david@designadecade.com.

DISCLAIMER

The author has made every effort to ensure that the information in this book was correct at the time of publication. However, the author and publisher accept no liability for any loss, damage or disruption incurred by the reader or any other person arising from any action taken or not taken based on the content of this book. The author recommends seeking third party advice and considering all options prior to making any decision or taking action in regard to the content of this book.

www.ingramcontent.com/pod-product-compliance
Ingram Content Group UK Ltd.
Pitfield, Milton Keynes, MK11 3LW, UK
UKHW022215230426
12048UKWH00016BA/859